Grateful acknowledgment is made to the following publishers, authors, and agents for their permission to reprint copyrighted material. Any adaptations are noted in the individual acknowledgments and are made with the full knowledge and approval of the authors or their representatives. Every effort has been made to locate all copyright proprietors; any errors or omissions in copyright notice are inadvertent and will be corrected in future printings as they are discovered.

"By Myself" from *HONEY, I LOVE and Other Love Poems* by Eloise Greenfield, pictures by Diane and Leo Dillon. (Thomas Y. Crowell) Copyright © 1978 by Eloise Greenfield, illustrations copyright 1978 by Diane and Leo Dillon. Reprinted by permission of Harper & Row, Publishers, Inc., and of the author's agents, Marie Brown Associates.

"The End" from *Now We Are Six* by A. A. Milne. Copyright © 1927 by E.P. Dutton, renewed 1955 by A. A. Milne. Reprinted by permission of the American publishers, E.P. Dutton, a division of NAL Penguin Inc., of the Canadian publishers, McClelland and Stewart, Toronto, and of the British publishers, Methuen Children's Books, a division of Associated Book Publishers (U.K.) Ltd., London.

Fix-It by David McPhail, text and art copyright © 1984 by David McPhail. Slightly adapted and reprinted by permission of the American publisher, E.P. Dutton, a division of Penguin Books USA Inc., and of the British publisher, Century Hutchinson Limited.

"The Hare and the Tortoise" adapted by Ramón Martinez, © 1989 by Silver, Burdett & Ginn Inc.

"Hippo Makes a Wish" excerpt adapted from *Hippo Lemonade* by Mike Thaler. Pictures by Maxie Chambliss. Text copyright © 1986 by Mike Thaler. Illustrations copyright © 1986 by Maxie Chambliss. Reprinted by permission of Harper & Row, Publishers, Inc., of the author's agents, Axelrod Rosenblum, and of the artist's agent, Jane Feder.

Acknowledgments continue on page 224, which constitutes an extension of this copyright page.

WORLD OF READING

MAKE A WISH

P. David Pearson   Dale D. Johnson

Theodore Clymer   Roselmina Indrisano   Richard L. Venezky

James F. Baumann   Elfrieda Hiebert   Marian Toth

Consulting Authors

Carl Grant   Jeanne Paratore

SILVER BURDETT & GINN

NEEDHAM, MA • MORRISTOWN, NJ

ATLANTA, GA • CINCINNATI, OH • DALLAS, TX

MENLO PARK, CA • DEERFIELD, IL

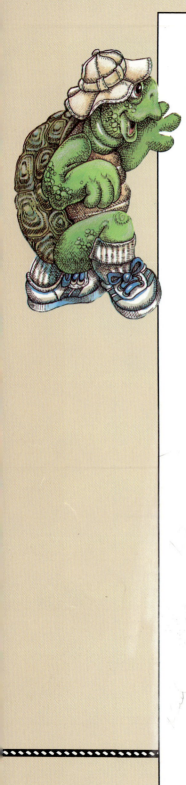

ALL ABOUT ANIMALS

UNIT ONE

then read Polar Bears - Mrs. Greßby

4

UNIT TWO

6

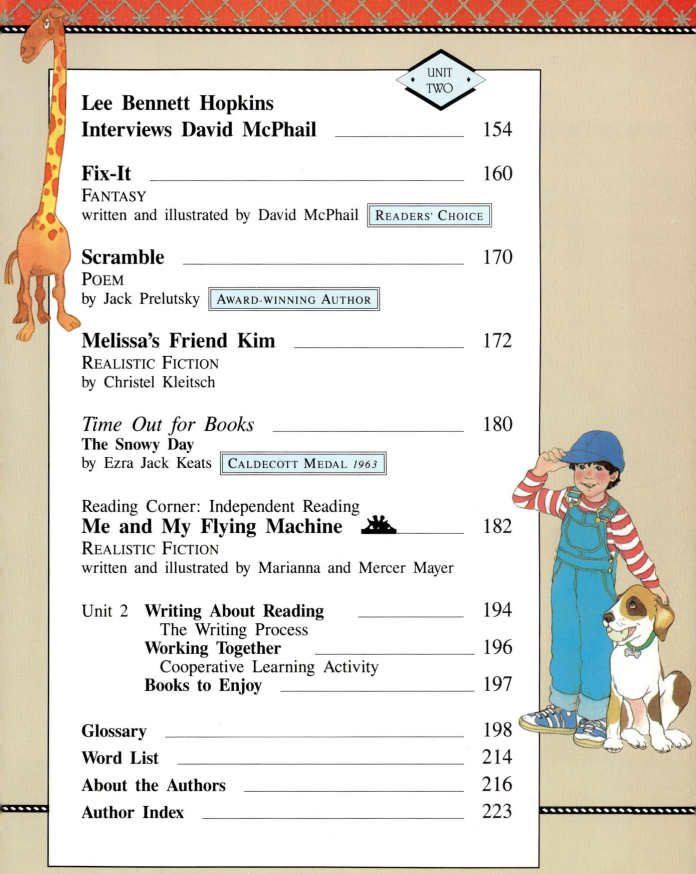

ALL ABOUT ANIMALS

*S*ome animals are real, and some are make-believe.

Why do we like stories about animals?

CAROUSEL HORSE,
wood carving by Illions,
American, c. 1923

A Morning in Fall
by Reeve Lindbergh

Many kinds of animals live on a farm. Early in the morning, some animals are already busy.

This is the farm on a morning in fall.
The sun has come over the hill.
Come and see who is sleeping and who is awake,
When the farm in the morning looks still.

Puppies will sleep this morning in fall.
Puppies sleep late on the farm.
One sleeping brother stays close to his mother.
It makes him feel happy and warm.

The cat is not sleeping this morning in fall.
The cat sees the cows going out.
She likes the warm sun on a morning that's fun.
She likes to be up and about.

Cows are not sleeping this morning in fall.
In the morning the cows go outside.

Take a calf for a run
　　and have all kinds of fun.
Take him back to his
　　warm mother's side.

15

Sheep are not sleeping this
    morning in fall.
You can run with the
    sheep down the hill.
You may find one sheep who
    is so good and so kind,
When you give her a hug
    she stays still.

16

Pigs are not sleeping this morning in fall.
Pigs like to play in the sun.
They play with their mother and play with
    each other.
These pigs all want to have fun.

This is the farm on a morning in fall,
When the sun has come over the hill.
You have seen who is sleeping and
   who is awake,
When the farm in the morning looks still.

Reader's Response

Tell the noises you might hear on
this farm in the morning in fall.

A Morning in Fall

Thinking It Over

1. How did the farm look in the morning?
2. Which animals were awake in the morning? Which animals were still sleeping?
3. What season of the year is it? How do you know?

Writing to Learn

THINK AND DECIDE   Whose eyes are closed this morning in fall? Draw a picture. Show someone or something who might be sleeping.

WRITE   Write what you see in your picture.

Asking Questions

How can you remember a story? One way is to ask questions. Two good questions to ask are, "Who is in the story?" and "What are the people or animals in the story doing?"

The picture below is from "A Morning in Fall."

Puppies will sleep this morning in fall.

Puppies sleep late on the farm.

One sleeping brother stays close to his mother.

It makes him feel happy and warm.

Who is in the story? What are they doing?
Does answering questions help you remember
the story?

Next you will read "Who Took the Farmer's
Hat?" Ask yourself, "Who is in the story?" and
"What are the people or animals doing?"

◆◆◆ The writing connection can be found on
page 53.

Who Took the Farmer's Hat?

by Joan Nödset

These animals see many things,
but not the farmer's hat.

The farmer had a hat,
an old brown hat.
Oh, how he liked that old brown hat!

But the wind took it,
and away it went.

So the farmer had to look for it.
He looked and he looked and he looked.
No old brown hat.

He saw Squirrel.
"Squirrel, did you see
my old brown hat?" said the farmer.

"No," said Squirrel.
"I saw a fat round brown bird.
A bird with no wings."

Who is
in this
story?

What are
they
doing?

23

The farmer saw Mouse.
"Mouse, did you see
my old brown hat?" said the farmer.

"No," said Mouse.
"I saw a big round brown mouse hole in
the grass.
I ran to it, but away it went." ◆◈▶

◆◈▶
**What is
the farmer
doing?**

24

The farmer saw Goat.
"Goat, did you see
my old brown hat?" said the farmer.

"No," said Goat.
"I saw a funny round brown pot.
I was going to eat it,
but the wind took that pot away."

The farmer saw Bird.
"Bird, did you take
my old brown hat?" said the farmer.

"No," said Bird.
"I saw this nice round brown
nest, but no hat."

The farmer looked
at the nest in the tree.
A nice old round brown nest.

Bird was in it.
And an egg was in it.

"Oh, my!" said the farmer.

"Like it?" said Bird.

"I like it," said the farmer.
"Oh, yes, I like that nice round brown nest.
It looks a little like my old brown hat.
But I see it is a nice round brown nest."

What
are the
animals
doing?

27

◄◆►
Who took the farmer's hat?

The farmer has a new brown hat.
Oh, how he likes that new brown hat!
And how Bird likes that old brown nest! **◄◆►**

◆ LIBRARY LINK ◆

Look in your library for more books by Joan Nŏdset. She wrote Come Here, Cat *and* Go Away, Dog.

Reader's Response

What part of this story surprised you?

Who Took the Farmer's Hat?

◆ Thinking It Over

1. How did the farmer lose his hat?
2. What did the goat think the farmer's hat was?
3. Is this story real or make-believe? How do you know?
4. Why do you think the bird used the hat for a nest?

◆ Writing to Learn

THINK AND IMAGINE   If you saw the farmer's hat, what would it look like to you? On a sheet of paper, draw what you think it would look like.

WRITE   Look at your picture. Label the things you see.

Magazine
News About Reading

Reading ABC Books

When you learned your ABCs, you may have used an ABC book. Look at these pictures from alphabet books. They show pictures of animals. The name of the animal begins with the letter in the picture.

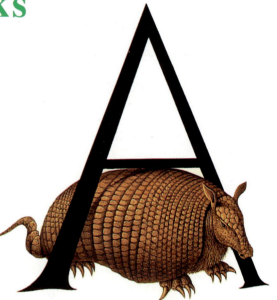

armadillo

The bear is playing a banjo under the letter **B**.

30

F f

F was once a little fish
Fishy
Wishy
Squishy
Fishy
In a Dishy
Little Fish!

You already know that **fish** begins with the letter **f**. But this ABC book has a silly poem about the fish. Wouldn't it be fun to read a book like this?

Ss

s s

Swan

This ABC book shows the letter in the shape of an animal. Do you think a swan is a good shape for the letter **S**?

☞ **These ABC books show animal pictures. But other alphabet books show different pictures. The next time you are in the library, see how many different alphabet books you can find.**

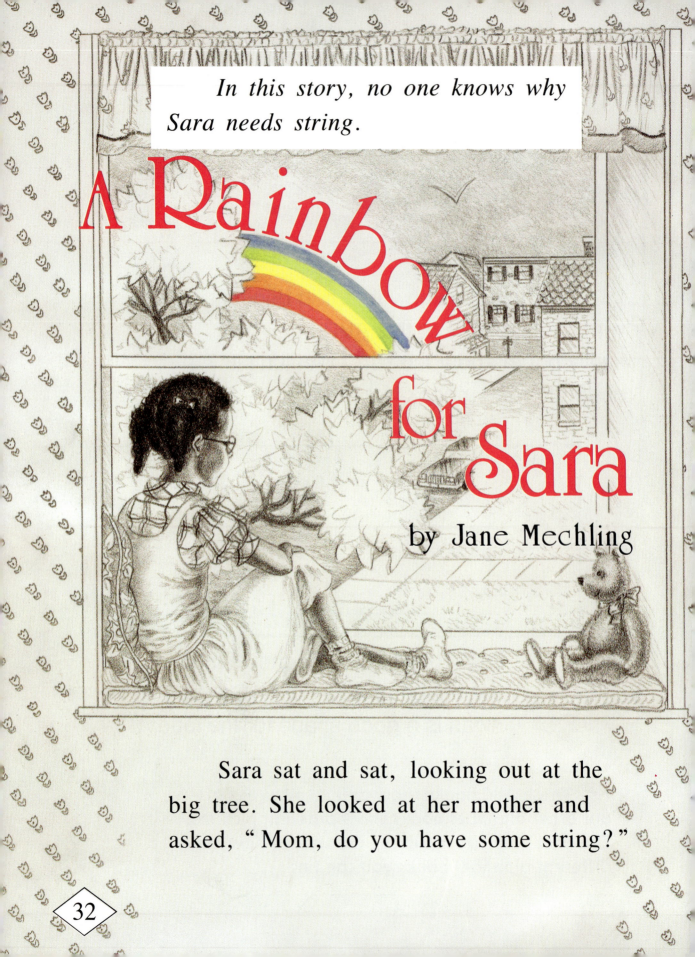

In this story, no one knows why
Sara needs string.

A Rainbow for Sara

by Jane Mechling

Sara sat and sat, looking out at the
big tree. She looked at her mother and
asked, "Mom, do you have some string?"

"Yes, here is some red string,"
said Sara's mother. "Is it for
your hair?"

"No," said Sara. "It's not
for my hair."

"I know," said Mother. "You
are going to fix something with it."

"No," said Sara. "You'll see."

Sara saw that her father had some string, too. She asked him for it.

"Here you are," said her father. "Do you need it to put around a box?"

"No," said Sara. "You'll see."

"I know," said Father. "You are going to fly your kite with it."

"No," Sara said. "I am thinking of something else."

Sara ran outside to play with Peter and Anna.

"I am keeping string in a box," said Sara.

"I have some green string in my pocket. You may have it," said Peter.

"You are keeping string?" said Anna. "What are you going to do with all that string? Will you and your cat play with it?"

"No," said Sara. "You'll see."

Soon Sara had all the string she needed. She had red string, orange string, green string, and yellow string. She had purple string, too! Sara put all her string near the big tree and waited.

She waited and waited. Then she waited some more. She waited until it was time for bed.

In the morning, Sara's mom asked,
"Where is all your string?"

"Come with me," said Sara.
She got her dad, and Peter and
Anna, too.

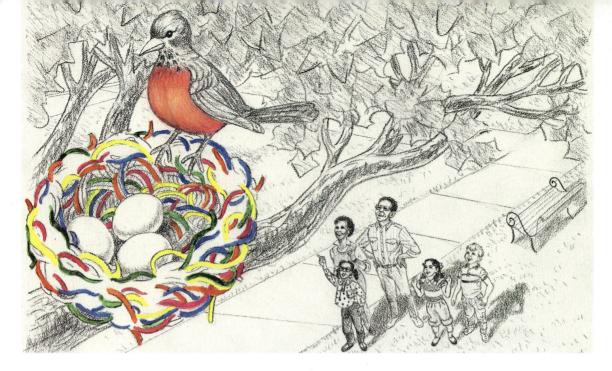

"Look!" said Sara.

"Oh my!" said Sara's dad.
"Your string helped a bird make
her nest."

Sara's mother said, "And look!
The bird made a rainbow for Sara!"

Reader's Response

How would you help birds make
a nest?

A Rainbow for Sara

Thinking It Over

1. What was Sara collecting?
2. Why did Sara ask everybody for string?
3. Do you think Sara was helping the bird? What makes you think so?
4. What was Sara's rainbow?

Writing to Learn

THINK AND DECIDE   Sara uses string in many ways. How do you use string?

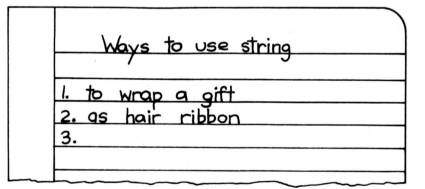

Ways to use string

1. to wrap a gift
2. as hair ribbon
3.

WRITE   Take out a sheet of paper. Make a list like Sara's list above. Your list will tell how you use string.

How to Help Make a Bird's Nest

by Marion de Barenne

In the spring, birds look for things to make nests. Would you like to help? Here is a way you can.

Tie two or three pine cones together like this.

Cut some string.
Put it on the pine cones like this.

Then tie the pine cones to a tree.
The birds will take the string
to make a nest!

When You Talk to a Monkey

When you talk to a monkey
    He seems very wise.
He scratches his head,
    And he blinks both his eyes;
But he won't say a word.
    He just swings on a rail
And makes a big question mark
    Out of his tail.

Rowena Bennett

Polar Bear Leaps

written by Derek Hall
illustrated by John Butler

*Animals can live anywhere. Meet
an animal that lives where it is always
cold.*

It is time for Polar Bear to come
out of the den where he was born.
For the first time he plays outside
in the snow.

As his mother eats, Polar Bear
runs off. The small bear stands up
on his back legs to look out over
the ice. Then, the ice breaks!

A small bit of ice takes Polar Bear
away from his mother. He sees his
mother and calls out to her for help.

Mother Bear calls back as she runs
to him. The small bear leaps over the
hole in the ice. His back legs slip
into the water.

Just in time Polar Bear's mother
grabs him by the neck. The water drips
off him as she pulls him from the water.
Polar Bear is safe now.

Now it is time for Polar Bear
to eat. Mother Bear feeds him.
Then he snuggles up close to her
and sleeps.

Reader's Response

Do you think Polar Bear should
have run off by himself? Tell why or
why not.

Polar Bear Leaps

Thinking It Over

1. Why did the ice begin to break?
2. What does Polar Bear need to learn before he grows up?
3. How did the story end?
4. Polar Bear lives in a place where it is always cold. How do you know this?

Writing to Learn

THINK AND TELL   Think about ''Polar Bear Leaps.'' *Who* was in the story? What did they do? Look at the words below.

Who?	Did What?
Little Polar Bear	leaped.
Polar Bear's Mother	saved him.

WRITE   Write one or two sentences. Tell *who* did what in this story.

53

LITERATURE LINK

What is a play?

Did you know that a story can be told in many ways? One way is to act it out. When you act out a story, it is called a play.

Here is a picture of some children in a play. They act out a story as people listen and watch.

Did you know that puppet shows, most movies, and many TV shows are kinds of plays?

The next story is written as a play. You will see pictures of children acting out the story. They are called players. As you read the play, think about which player is speaking.

The
Three Little Pigs

adapted by Adam Burdick

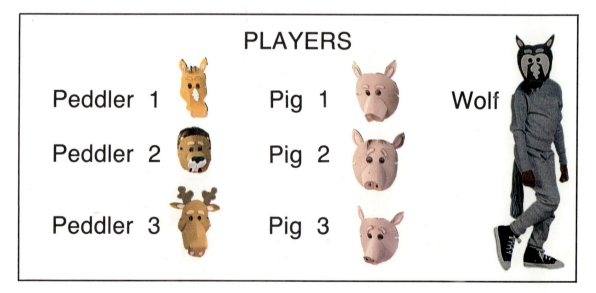

PLAYERS

Peddler 1   Pig 1   Wolf

Peddler 2   Pig 2

Peddler 3   Pig 3

There are different ways to keep a wolf away.

Peddler 1: Straw! Straw for sale!
One corncob for a bale!

Peddler 2: Get your sticks! Just cut!
Sticks for sale!

Peddler 3: Bricks! Just six corncobs!

Pig 1: I think I will make my house
from straw. Straw is strong.
Please give me some straw.

Pig 2: I think I will make my house
from sticks. Sticks are
stronger than straw. Please
give me some sticks.

Pig 3: I will make my house from
bricks. Bricks cost more,
but they are the strongest
of all. Please give me
some bricks.

Pig 1: What a fine house
        I have made.

Wolf: Knock, knock.

Pig 1: Who is it?

Wolf: It's a friend. Little pig,
       little pig, please, let me in.

Pig 1: Not by the hair on my
chinny chin chin.

Wolf: Then I'll huff, and I'll puff,
and I'll blow your house in!

Pig 1: Help! Help! The wolf is
here. I will run to my
sister's house. Her stick house
will keep me safe.

Pig 1:   Sister, please, let me in!
The wolf blew my house
down!

Pig 2:   Please, come in. My house
of sticks will keep you safe.

Wolf: Knock, knock.

Pig 2:   Who is it?

Wolf: It's a friend. Little pig, little pig, please, let me in.

Pigs 1 & 2: Not by the hairs on our chinny chin chins.

Wolf: Then I'll huff, and I'll puff, and I'll blow your house in!

Pig 2: We can run to our big sister's house. Her brick house will keep us safe.

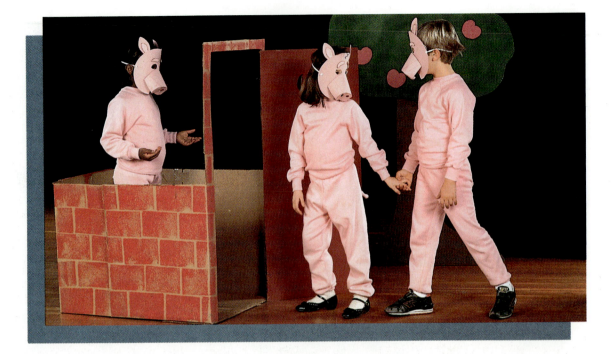

Pigs 1 & 2: Knock, knock.

Pig 3: Can I help you?

Pig 1: The wolf blew down
my straw house.

Pig 2: The wolf blew down
my stick house.

Pigs 1 & 2: Can we come in with you?

Pig 3: Please, do come in. You will
be safe in my strong brick
house.

Wolf: Knock, knock.

Pig 3: Who is it?

Wolf: It's a friend. Little pig,
little pig, please, let me in.

Pigs 1, 2, Not by the hairs on our
and 3: chinny chin chins.

Wolf: Then I'll huff, and I'll puff,
and I'll blow your house in.

Pig 3: My house is too strong.
         You cannot blow it in.

Wolf: Huff, puff! Huff, puff!
         Huff, puff! Huff, puff!
         Just one more time will
         blow this house down!
         HUFFFFFFF, PUFFFFFF.
         Oh, I give up! This house
         is too strong!

Reader's Response

Would you like to live in a
house made from straw or sticks?
Tell why.

The Three Little Pigs

◆ Thinking It Over

1. What do you think Pig 1 and Pig 2 will use to build their houses next time? Tell why you think this.
2. How are straw and sticks alike?
3. Which Pig's house did the wolf knock at first, second, and last?

◆ Writing to Learn

THINK AND PRETEND   Pretend that you are going to make a new house. What would you use to build it? Draw a picture of your new house.

WRITE   Write what would happen if the wolf came to your house.

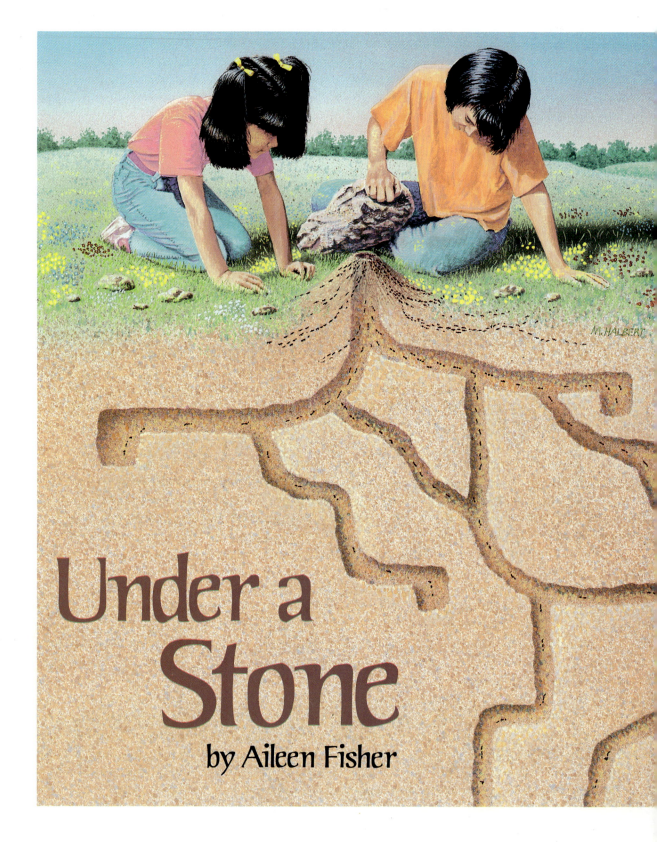

Under a
Stone

by Aileen Fisher

In the middle of a meadow
we turned up a stone
and saw a little village
we never had known,
with little streets and tunnels
and ant-folk on the run,
all frightened and excited
by the sudden burst of sun.

We watched them rushing headlong,
and then put back the stone
to cover up the village
we never had known,
to roof away the tunnels
where ants were on the run
before they got all sunburned
in the bright hot sun.

People build and live in many
different kinds of homes. Animals do, too.

A World of Animals

by Susan Schroeder

The world is home for many animals.
All animals need a place to live.

You can find animals under the
ground, in the sky, and in the water.
Animals live all around us.

Turtles live on land and in water.
All turtles have a shell. The shell is
a home for the turtle. Some turtles can
hide in their shells.

Ducks make their homes near water.
Ducks swim in the water and look
for food. They make nests out of grass
and mud near the water. The grass
around the water hides their nests.

Some rabbits make their homes in meadows. They dig holes under the ground. Then they make nests out of their fur. Under the ground, the rabbits are warm and safe.

Many birds make their homes in trees. They fly to the ground to find things for their nests. They take the grass, sticks, and mud to the trees to make their nests. Birds are safe in their homes in the trees.

All animals need a place to live. There are many animal homes in the world. Look around you. What animals live near you?

Do you think a turtle would want to live in a duck's nest? Tell why or why not.

A World of Animals

Thinking It Over

1. Name three places where animals make their homes.
2. How are the homes of a duck and a rabbit alike? How are they different?
3. Name two things that help you know that this is a real story. What makes you think so?

Writing to Learn

THINK AND REMEMBER Think of the most interesting animal that you have ever seen. Draw a picture of your animal in a home.

WRITE Label the parts of your picture.

Rabbits are usually faster than turtles, but not always.

The Hare and the Tortoise

adapted by Ramón Martinez

Tortoise went out for a walk in the city. When he came to the park, he saw his friend, Hare.

"It is nice to see you, friend," said Hare. "Where are you going?"

"I am out for a walk," said Tortoise.

"That's nice," said Hare.

"Will you walk with me, Hare?" said Tortoise.

"Oh, no!" said Hare. "Rabbits don't walk. Rabbits run as fast as the wind!"

"As fast as the wind?" asked Tortoise.

"As fast as the wind," said Hare.
"Don't you believe me? Then I'll
show you. Will you race with me
around the city and back to the park?"

"I don't mind if I do,"
said Tortoise. "You may be as fast as
the wind, but you aren't the best."

So Hare and Tortoise had a race.
Off ran Hare as fast as the wind.

Now Hare was fast, but not very wise. He did not believe that Tortoise could win the race. So when he came to a bench at a bus stop, he sat down.

"I have lots of time," he said, "and I am tired. I will take a little nap."

So Hare went to sleep.

Now Tortoise was not very fast,
but he did not stop. On and on
he went. Tortoise was very tired,
but he did not stop.

Tortoise came to the bus stop.
There he saw his friend, Hare.

"Oh, my," Tortoise said.
"Hare is sleeping. I'll keep going.
I know I can win this race."

When Hare woke up he looked
for Tortoise. Tortoise was not in
back of him. Hare did not see
Tortoise at all.

"Where is Tortoise?" said Hare.
"I will go to the park. I will win
the race."

Hare ran to the park. Tortoise
was waiting for him.

"You have won the race!" said Hare to Tortoise. "I can run as fast as the wind! How did you win the race?"

"You may run faster, but I do not stop when I run," said Tortoise. "You cannot win a race if you stop."

"I think I will stop now. May I sit with you on this bench?" said Hare.

"I don't mind if you do," said Tortoise.

Reader's Response

Did you want the Hare or the Tortoise to win the race? Tell why.

The Hare and the Tortoise

Thinking It Over

1. Who was faster at the beginning of the race? Who was faster at the end?
2. How did Tortoise win the race?
3. What might have happened if Hare had not taken a nap? Why do you think this?

Writing to Learn

THINK AND DECIDE Hare and Tortoise had a race. Draw a picture to show your favorite part of this race.

WRITE Write a sentence to tell why Tortoise won the race.

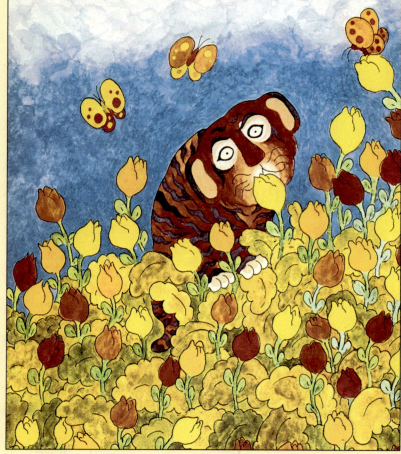

Leo the Late Bloomer

BY ROBERT KRAUS · PICTURES BY JOSE ARUEGO

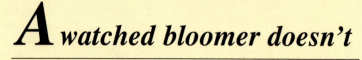

A *watched bloomer doesn't* **bloom.** from *Leo the Late Bloomer* by Robert Kraus

Pictures by Jose Aruego

Jose Aruego drew the pictures for *Leo the Late Bloomer*. Jose loves to draw funny animals. When he was a boy, his family had three horses and seven dogs. They had six cats and three pigs. They had frogs, tadpoles, and a duck, too.

When Jose grew up, he became an artist. He didn't forget all those animals. Now he draws funny animals that make him laugh.

If you read *Leo the Late Bloomer*, you will meet Leo and the other colorful animals. Find out what Leo does when nobody is watching.

Mercy, Percy!

by Else Holmelund Minarik

"Parsnips," said Percy, drumming on the table. "I want parsnips. I want to eat parsnips."

"Mother," said Percy. "Will you cook parsnips for me?"

"Mercy, Percy!" said mother. "We have no parsnips. Will bark bits do?"

No, Percy did not want bark bits.
Percy wanted parsnips.

"I want parsnips," said Percy.
He drummed on the table.

"Stop drumming the table!" said Mother. "Here is your grandpa."

"Grandpa, Percy wants to eat parsnips. I have no parsnips. Do you have any parsnips?" said Mother.

"Oh, yes!" said Grandpa. "I have fine parsnips in my garden. My parsnips are the best! Come with me, Percy. We will get the parsnips. Then we can help mother cook them for you."

They came to the garden. Percy looked about. He saw some strawberries. He ate them.

And he saw some gooseberries, some big fine gooseberries. He began to eat the gooseberries.

Now gooseberry bushes are sticky.
But that did not stop Percy.

"I like it here," said Percy.
"I like to be stuck in sticky bushes,
with big fine gooseberries to eat."

Percy ate a lot of gooseberries.

Grandpa pulled up his parsnips.
And then he pulled Percy out of the
bushes.

"Percy," said Grandpa, "you will
have a gooseberry tummy ache."

Grandpa was right. Percy did have
a gooseberry tummy ache.

Percy cried, "All I wanted was
parsnips!"

Mother said, "Parsnips will have to
wait." She patted Percy's tummy.

Percy waited.

Then he was fine. His tummy ache went away.

"I am fine now, Mother," he said. "I am ready for parsnips."

"Good for you," said Mother.

She cooked the parsnips and Percy ate them.

"Mercy, Percy!" said mother. "Do you want more?"

"Yes," said Percy.

"I'll have some too," said Grandpa.

Mother said, "Well then, so will I."

So they had a family parsnip party!

Percy did not get a parsnip tummy ache.
Not Percy! But then, no one ever gets a
parsnip tummy ache.

Reader's Response

Do you believe Percy will behave
differently when he goes into the
garden tomorrow?

Writing an Ad

You have just read some stories about animals. Pretend one of those animals is yours. One day your pet gets lost. How could you let people know that you have lost your pet? One way is to write a ''lost and found'' ad.

Getting Ready

A ''lost and found'' ad tells what you have lost and how people can return it. Use the box below to plan your ad.

Question	Your answer
1. What kind of pet have you lost?	
2. What is your pet's name?	
3. What does it look like?	
4. What should people do if they find it?	

Writing

Now write your "lost and found" ad. You may want to draw a picture of your pet.

Listening to My Writing

Read your ad to a partner. Does your partner know what you lost and what to do if your pet is found? Add more words if you need to.

Sharing

Put your ad on a bulletin board in your classroom.

Making Hidden Pictures

You have read about all kinds of animals. Some live on land, and some live in water. Today you and a friend will draw a picture together. Then you will hide some animals in your picture.

Remember to:

♦ Take turns sharing ideas.

♦ Use quiet voices when you talk.

First, get the things you will need to make your picture. Talk about what to draw. Then draw the picture together. When your picture is done, draw some hidden animals in it. Can a friend find the animals?

BOOKS TO ENJOY

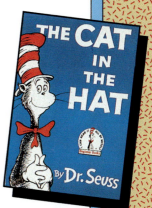

The Cat in the Hat by Dr. Seuss *(Random House, 1957)*. A special ''cat'' who wears a tall red and white striped hat visits two children on a rainy day.

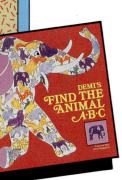

Demi's Find the Animal A·B·C by Demi *(Grosset & Dunlap, 1985)*. You will have fun trying to find the animals in this ABC book. Every letter of the alphabet has a matching animal.

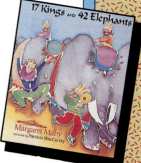

17 Kings and 42 Elephants by Margaret Mahy *(Dial Books, 1987)*. Follow 17 kings and 42 elephants as they walk through the jungle singing. Several jungle animals join in the fun.

LET'S PRETEND

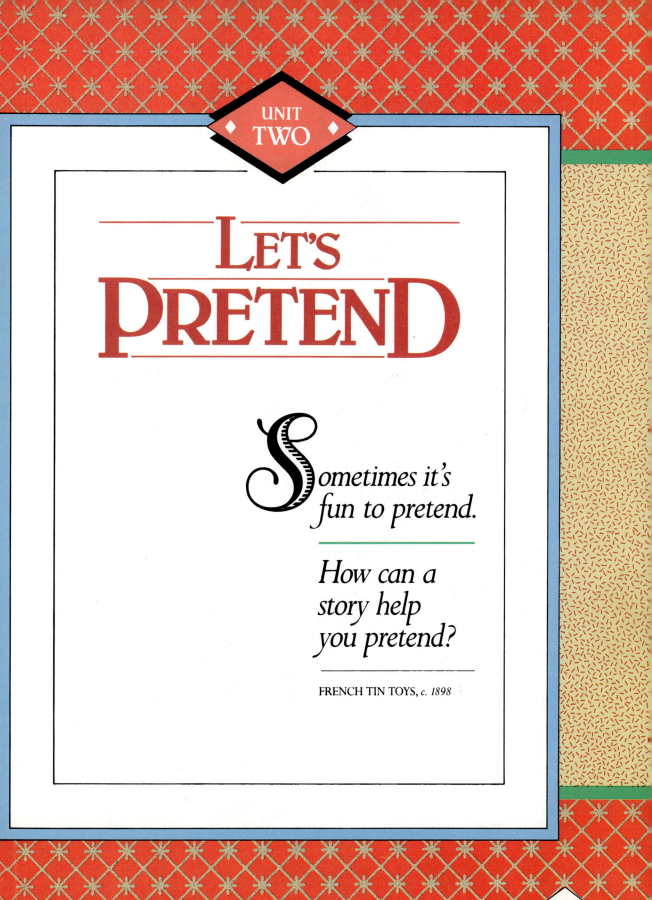

*S*ometimes it's
fun to pretend.

*How can a
story help
you pretend?*

FRENCH TIN TOYS, *c. 1898*

I Want to Be Big, NOW!

written and illustrated
by Bernard Wiseman

Friends help each other.
June's friends help her pretend.

June was sad. "The kids over there say that I can't play with them. I think they're being rude," she said. "They say that I am too little. I wish I could be bigger."

"Can't you wait?" said Pat. "Our moms were little. Our dads were little, too. Now they are big. If you wait, you'll get big, too."

"But I don't want to wait,"
said June. "I want to be big NOW!"

"I know how to help you,"
said Jeff. "Come with me to my house."

Jeff got out some food.

"Here," said Jeff. "Eat all
of this. My dad always tells me
if I eat all my vegetables, I will
grow to be big and strong. Maybe
if you eat all of this, you'll get
bigger and stronger faster."

"There," she said. "I can't eat any more. But I don't feel any bigger!"

"You don't look any bigger," said Greg.

"But I want to be big NOW," said June.

"I know what we can do," said Pat. "We can help you to look big. Come with me."

"Here, June. Put on
my mom's things," said Pat.
"Now you look big! See?"

"See?" said June. "I can't see!
The hat is over my eyes. I could fall.
This won't work!"

"I know," said Greg.
"Come with me."

"Here," said Greg. "Stand on these. These will make you big."

"I can see that I am bigger," said June. "But they are hard to walk with. It will be hard to ride my bicycle. These won't work. Maybe I was wrong. Maybe I can't be big now."

"My gram always tells me that it takes a big person to admit when she's wrong," said Pat.

"You know what that means, June?" said Jeff. "You ARE big, and you are big NOW!"

Reader's Response

Do you think June had good friends? Tell why or why not.

I Want to Be Big, **NOW!**

◆ Thinking It Over

1. What three steps did June's friends take to try to help her?
2. Why didn't eating or dressing up help June to be bigger?
3. Did June show that she was big? How do you know this?

◆ Writing to Learn

THINK AND DISCOVER   June thought trying on a grown-up's clothes made her look older. Draw a picture to show what you would look like in a grown-up's clothes.

WRITE   Look at your picture. Do you feel older? Write how you feel.

Then

When you can catch
And throw a ball,
And spell
Cat,
Dog,
And Pig,
Then you have finished
Being small
And started
Being Big.

Dorothy Aldis

The End

When I was One,
I had just begun.

When I was Two,
I was nearly new.

When I was Three,
I was hardly Me.

When I was Four,
I was not much more.

When I was Five,
I was just alive.

But now I am Six, I'm as clever as clever.
So I think I'll be six now for ever and ever.

A. A. Milne

A mouse finds a clever
way to solve a problem.

The
Wishing
Well

from *Mouse Tales*

written and illustrated
by ARNOLD LOBEL

A mouse once found
a wishing well.
"Now all of my wishes
can come true!"
she cried.
She threw a penny
into the well
and made a wish.
"OUCH!"
said the wishing well.

115

The next day
the mouse came back
to the well.
She threw a penny
into the well
and made a wish.
"OUCH!" said the well.

The next day
the mouse came back again.
She threw a penny
into the well.
" I wish this well
would not say ouch,"
she said.
" OUCH!" said the well.
" That hurts!"

"What shall I do?"
cried the mouse.
"My wishes
will never ever
come true this way!"

The mouse ran home.
She took the pillow
from her bed.
"This may help,"
said the mouse,
and she ran back
to the well.

The mouse threw the pillow
into the well.
Then she threw
a penny into the well
and made a wish.

" Ah . That feels
much better ! "
said the well .
" Good ! " said the mouse .
" Now I can start wishing . "

After that day
the mouse made many wishes
by the well.
And every one of them
came true.

Reader's Response

How would you have solved the
mouse's problem?

The Wishing Well

◆ Thinking It Over

1. What did the mouse want to do when she saw the wishing well?
2. How did the well feel after the mouse threw the pillow in? How can you tell?
3. What wishes did the mouse make?
4. Name one thing that tells you that this story is make-believe.

◆ Writing to Learn

THINK AND IMAGINE   Pretend that you are at a wishing well. Show what you would wish for. Draw a picture of it.

WRITE   Tell about your picture.

LITERATURE LINK

What helps you read new words?

This little part of "The Wishing Well" has some new words in it.

She threw a penny
into the well
and made a wish.

Do you ever get stuck on a word you don't know, like *threw* or *penny*, when you read? Lots of people do. If you get stuck, there are some things you can do.

Try These Tips

You know a lot about letters and the sounds they stand for. When you come to a new word, look for letters whose sounds you know. Put the sounds together to sound out the whole word.

When you think you know the word, read the sentence again. Think about the story. Ask yourself, "Does this word make sense here?"

Look at the pictures, too. Sometimes the pictures can help you.

Now you try:

If I were an airplane,
I'd fly fast.
I'd fly so fast no one
could see me.

Remember these tips when you read "The Story Game."

In many games, you have to pretend. These children pretend to see a dinosaur.

The Story Game

by Steven Kroll

I was on my way
to get some peaches
and I heard a yell from
Jimmy's house. So I ran to
his house and there were Jimmy
and Peggy and Lee and a big
tyrannosaurus stuck on the stairs.
Everyone pulled and pushed and
pushed and pulled.
Then, the tyrannosaurus sneezed
and everyone flew out the door.
And Rusty said . . .

I was waiting
for the bus,
and Jimmy and Peggy
and Lee and Billy and
Alice and the tyrannosaurus
and I all got on.
Everyone else had
to get off.

And Stuart said. . .

RUSTY

STUART

I was
on the seesaw
at the playground,
and this tyrannosaurus
came running up and
sat down on the other end
and I flew into the air
and landed on his back.
And Joanne said . . .

STUART

JOANNE

I was
on the swings,
and Jimmy and Peggy
and all of my friends
came dashing by
with a tyrannosaurus.
And I jumped off
and ran after them.
And Lee said . . .

136

And then
the police came
and looked all over
the city,
but the tyrannosaurus
was gone!

Reader's Response

Pretend you could walk into the story and play a game. Which game would you like to play?

The Story Game

Thinking It Over

1. What did Joanne see?
2. How are these words alike: *Jimmy, Rusty, Lee,* and *Billy*?
3. If you were playing this game, what would you pretend to see?
4. The children were playing a game of pretend. How do you know?

Writing to Learn

THINK AND PRETEND
The children in " The Story Game " saw a tyrannosaurus. What animal would you like to see in a story? Draw a picture.
WRITE Tell about your picture. Write three things that your animal can do.

By Myself

written by Eloise Greenfield
illustrated by Diane and Leo Dillon

When I'm by myself
And I close my eyes
I'm a twin
I'm a dimple in a chin
I'm a room full of toys
I'm a squeaky noise
I'm a gospel song
I'm a gong
I'm a leaf turning red
I'm a loaf of brown bread
I'm a whatever I want to be
An anything I care to be
And when I open my eyes
What I care to be
Is me

140

141

Hippo wants to make a wish. His friends give him some ideas.

Hippo Makes a Wish

written by Mike Thaler
illustrated by Maxie Chambliss

Hippo opened his eyes.
"Today I would like
to make a wish," he said.
Hippo thought and thought and thought.
But he could not think of what
to wish for.

So he got out of the river
and went to see Snake.

"Snake," said Hippo,
"I would like to make a wish.
But I don't know what to wish for."
"Wish for bright colors, like mine,"
said Snake.
Hippo saw himself with bright colors
like Snake's.
"I don't think so," said Hippo.
And he went to see Monkey.

"Wish for a long tail like mine,"
said Monkey.
"Then we could swing
in the trees together."
"That's true," said Hippo.
Hippo saw himself
swinging in the trees.
"I don't think so," he said.
And he went to see Lion.

"Wish for a curly mane
like mine," said Lion.
Hippo saw himself
with a mane like Lion's.
"I don't think so," he said,
and he went to see Giraffe.

"You could see the tops of trees,"
said Giraffe, "with a neck
like mine."
"That's true," said Hippo.
Hippo saw himself
with a long neck like Giraffe's.
"I don't think so," said Hippo,
and he went to see Elephant.

"I know!" said Elephant.
"Wish for a nose just like mine."
Hippo saw himself
with Elephant's nose.
"I don't think so," he said,
and he went back to the river.

He closed his eyes.

"What are you doing?" asked Mole.

"I am wishing," said Hippo.

"What are you wishing for?" asked Mole.

"I am wishing to stay
just as I am," said Hippo.
Mole looked at Hippo.
Hippo looked at Mole.
Mole winked.
"Your wish has come true."

What would you have told Hippo
to wish for if you had been his friend?

Hippo Makes a Wish

◆ Thinking It Over

1. Whom did Hippo see first? Whom did he see last?
2. Where did Hippo live? What tells you this?
3. Why did Hippo wish to stay as he was?

◆ Writing to Learn

THINK AND PLAN Hippo wanted to make a wish. You can make a wish, too. Take out a sheet of paper and draw a ''wish'' on it.

WRITE What did you wish? Write a sentence about your wish.

Magazine
News About Reading

Words Are All Around Us

Look at these words and see how many of them you can read.

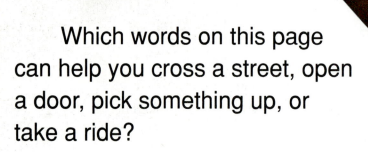

Which words on this page can help you cross a street, open a door, pick something up, or take a ride?

Here is a truck that carries bread and cake and ones that move heavy loads. How many other kinds of trucks can you find on your way to and from school?

Which words on this page can help you get to school, find your way if you get lost, or have a happy surprise party?

David McPhail

David McPhail makes picture books. He makes up the story and the drawings, too.

"I started to draw when I was two," Mr. McPhail said. "I drew pictures on brown bags. I drew pictures on anything I could find at home and at school."

Mr. McPhail said, "My mother liked my drawings a lot. She would hang them up around the house. My mother told my sister and brothers that we could be anything we wanted to be!"

Mr. McPhail has a house in New England. "I like books, tall trees, the warm sun, and the blue sky," he said. "I do not like snow, ice, and TV."

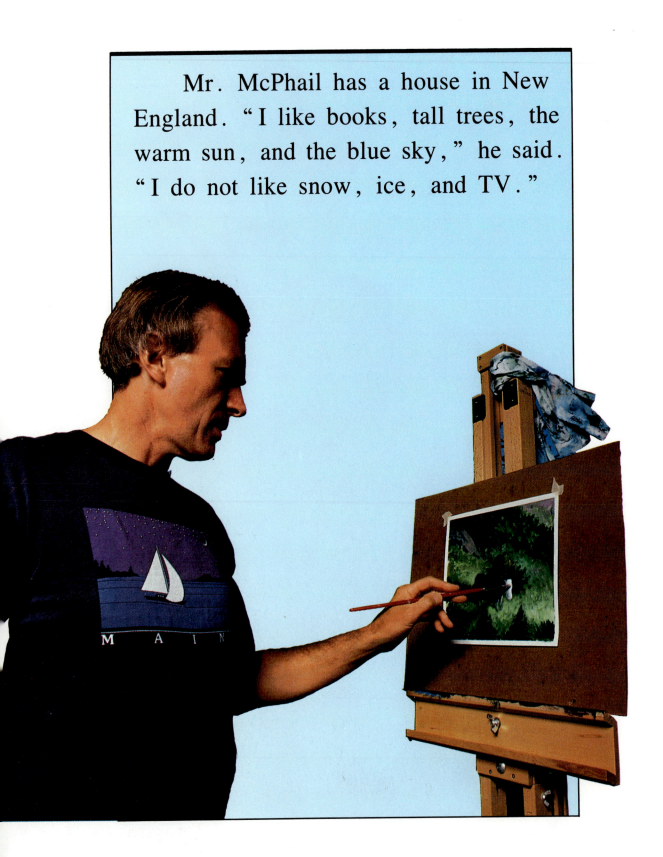

"I always have new stories in my mind," Mr. McPhail said. "When I sit in my car, I may think of anything. I may think of a pig in a truck. I may think of bears."

"One time I wanted to make a picture book about a bear. I made many drawings of bears," said Mr. McPhail.

When you read the next story, you will see some of Mr. McPhail's pictures of bears. After you have read it, you may want to look for some of his other books:

Henry Bear's Park
Pig Pig Grows Up
Adam's Smile

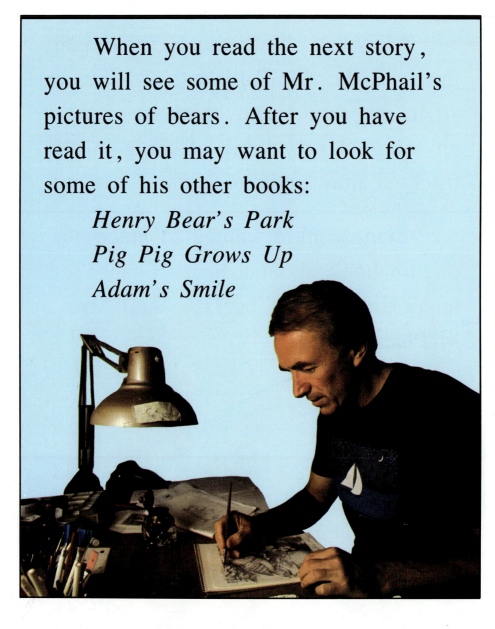

Reader's Response

David McPhail likes to draw pictures. What do you like to do?

SELECTION FOLLOW-UP

LEE BENNETT HOPKINS INTERVIEWS

David McPhail

◆ **Thinking It Over**

1. How does David McPhail make picture books?

2. Do you think David McPhail would like to live where it is always cold? How do you know?

3. In what way did David McPhail's mother help him to be who he is today?

◆ **Writing to Learn**

THINK AND CHOOSE David McPhail likes books, tall trees, the warm sun, and the blue sky. What do you like? Draw a picture of some of the things you like.

WRITE Label the things in your picture.

When the TV won't work, Emily
discovers another way to enjoy herself.

FIX-IT

written and illustrated
by David McPhail

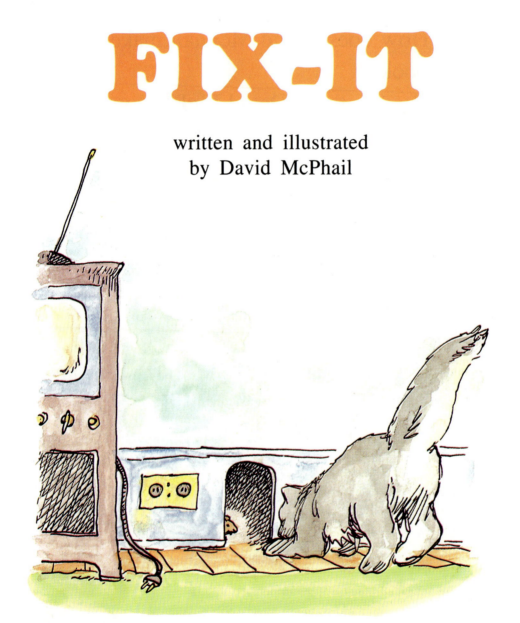

One morning Emma got up
early to watch television.
But the TV didn't work.

Emma asked her mother to fix it.
"Hurry, Mom!" she cried.
Emma's mother tried to fix it.
But she couldn't.

Emma's father tried.

But he couldn't fix it, either.

So he called the fix-it man.

"Please hurry," he said.

"It's an emergency!"

The fix-it man came right away.
He tried to fix the TV.
Emma's mother and father
tried to fix Emma.
Her father blew up a balloon . . .
until it popped.

Her mother sang a song.
So did the cat.
Her father pretended to be a horse—
but Emma didn't feel like riding.

Finally her mother read her a book.
"Read it again," said Emma
when her mother had finished.
"And again."
"And again."

"Now I'll read to Millie,"
said Emma.
And she went to her room.

Then her father found out what was
wrong with the TV.
"I fixed it!" he called.
But Emma didn't come out of her room.

She was too busy.

Reader's Response

What kinds of books can keep you
busy all day?

FIX-IT

◆ Thinking It Over

1. What did Emma's father and mother do to keep her busy when the TV didn't work?

2. Why didn't the TV work? How do you know?

3. Did Emma want to watch TV after her father fixed it? Tell why or why not.

◆ Writing to Learn

THINK AND DECIDE Make a book cluster for Emma. Draw Emma in a little circle. Then put in the names of your favorite books.

WRITE Send a note to Emma. Tell her about a book in your cluster.

Scramble

If the zebra were given
    the spots of the leopard
and the leopard
    the stripes of the zebra,
then the leopard would have to
    be renamed the zeopard,
and the zebra retitled the lebra.

And wouldn't we laugh
    if the gentle giraffe
swapped his neck for the
    hump on the camel?
For the camel would henceforth
    be called the camaffe,
the giraffe designated giramel.

It would be very funny,
　　if the ears of the bunny
were exchanged for
　　the horns of the sheep.
For the sheep would then surely
　　be known as the shunny,
and the bunny quite simply the beep.

Jack Prelutsky

171

Melissa likes to pretend.
Sometimes her mom and dad
pretend, too.

Melissa's Friend Kim

by Christel Kleitsch

"Good morning, Mom," said Melissa.

"Good morning, Melissa," said Mom.

"Say good morning to Kim,"
said Melissa.

"Who's Kim?" asked Mom.

"This is Kim. She's over here,"
said Melissa.

"Oh, I see," said Mom.
"Good morning, Kim."

"Watch out, Dad," said Melissa.
"Please, don't sit there."

"Why not?" asked Dad.

"Kim is sitting there," said Melissa.

"Who's Kim?" said Dad.

"This is my friend, Kim," said Melissa.
"She's going to eat breakfast with us."

"It's nice to meet you, Kim," said Dad.

"Mom, may Kim have some breakfast?"
asked Melissa.

"Let her have some of yours, Melissa,"
said Mom.

"Kim can't have this for breakfast,"
said Melissa.

"She can't?" said Mom. "What can
Kim have for breakfast?"

"She has ice cream," said Melissa.

"Ice cream for breakfast?" said Mom.

"Oh, yes," said Melissa.

"Didn't I get ice cream just the other day?" said Dad.

"Yes, you did," said Mom. "Would you both like some?"

"I believe I'll pass," said Dad.

"Both Kim and I would love some," said Melissa.

"Thanks, Mom," Melissa said. "This is good!"

"May Kim come for lunch tomorrow?" said Melissa.

"Sure she can," said Mom. "I'll make you both some spinach sandwiches."

"Spinach sandwiches?" said Melissa.

"Yes," said Mom. "Kim told me that's what she eats for lunch."

"Oh, no!" said Melissa. Then they all laughed.

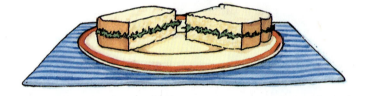

Reader's Response

Do you think Melissa and her parents had fun? Tell why or why not.

Melissa's Friend Kim

◆ **T**hinking It Over

1. Why did Dad start to sit where Kim sat?
2. How did Melissa's mom surprise her?
3. Where do you think Melissa's dad got the ice cream?
4. Could Kim be a real person? What makes you think so?

◆ **W**riting to Learn

THINK AND PRETEND   Think about what Melissa and Kim might say when they are given spinach sandwiches.

Melissa

Kim

WRITE   Copy the speech balloons. Write the words for Melissa and Kim.

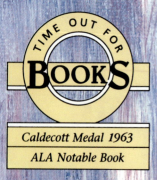

Caldecott Medal 1963
ALA Notable Book

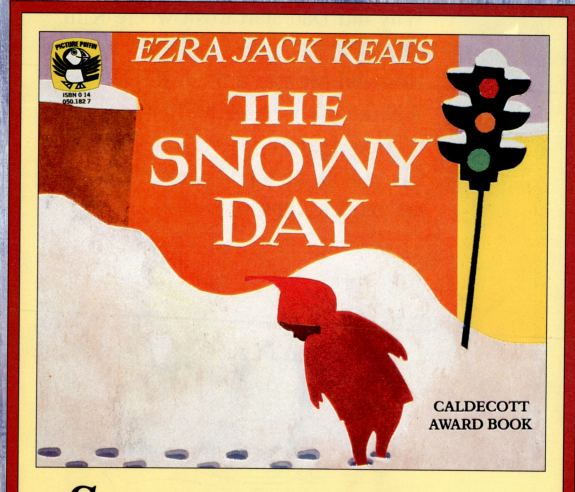

Snow had fallen during the night. It covered everything as far as he could see.

from *The Snowy Day* by Ezra Jack Keats

In the book *The Snowy Day*, a boy named Peter wakes up and looks out the window. He sees a brand new world. The whole city is covered in snow!

This really happened to Ezra Jack Keats, the author of *The Snowy Day*. He remembered days when the snow changed everything. And he knew how to tell a good story about it. He had been making up stories for his friends since he was nine.

Ezra Jack Keats drew the pictures for *The Snowy Day*, too. If you read this book, you will follow Peter through his very special, very snowy day.

ME and MY FLYING MACHINE

By MARIANNA and MERCER MAYER

Last summer I discovered an old
barn. It was full of great things.

There were boxes, pieces of wood.
There were even nails and a hammer.
I could build anything I wanted.
I'll build a flying machine, I thought,
and I started building.
I worked all day.

My flying machine was almost
finished but it was dinner time and I had
to wash the dog.

So I closed up the barn for the night. "Good-bye, flying machine. I'll finish you tomorrow," I said and went home.

That night I dreamed about my flying machine and how it would look when I was finished. It would be something tremendous. Smaller than a castle but bigger than a truck.

I finally decided on something smaller.
Besides, it would take me too long
to build a big flying machine.

There were so many things I could do.
I'd deliver mail to Eskimos and people
who never get mail.

I'd fly above the fog and rescue lost
boats at sea.

I'd carry mountain climbers to the
mountain top. So they wouldn't have
to spend so much time climbing.

Birds could rest on the wings, if they
were tired from flying around all day.

From high in my flying machine I could
see everything. So I'd always know where
everything was and I'd never get lost.

My flying machine would win first prize in every race.

And soon I'd have so many medals and trophies that I wouldn't know where to keep them.

I couldn't wait to finish my flying
machine. The next day I ran all the way
to the old barn.

Everything was just like I left it.

There was more work to do so I
nailed on another wing and some stuff.

I finished working on my flying machine but somehow it didn't look quite the way I thought it would.

There was a brush and some old paint cans lying around. So I used a little of each. It was just what my flying machine needed.

It looked better than I had imagined.
So I tied a rope on the front end to
pull my flying machine outside to dry.

It creaked and moaned
and started to shake as I pulled.

And then before I could pull it out of
the barn . . . my flying machine
fell apart.

Tomorrow I'll build a rowboat.

◆ Reader's Response

If you found a barn filled with
wood and things, what would you build?

Writing About a Make-Believe Friend

You read the story about Melissa and her make-believe friend, Kim. Pretend you have a make-believe friend.

Getting Ready

Close your eyes and think about your make-believe friend.

♦ Is it a boy or a girl or a pet?

♦ How old is your friend?

♦ What does your make-believe friend look like?

Writing

Open your eyes and draw what you saw. Then write about your friend. Copy and finish the sentences below.

My make-believe friend's name is _____.

I like my friend because _____.

My friend looks like _____.

My friend and I like to _____.

Listening to My Writing

Read what you wrote to a partner. Would you like to write anything more about your make-believe friend?

Sharing

Paste your picture and your writing onto a large sheet of paper. Show your story to your classmates.

Planning a Play
Without Words

Today you and a friend can work together.
You will put on a play that has no words.
Remember:

♦ Listen to your friend's ideas.
♦ Help each other practice.

Now think of some things that
the play could be about. You
might pretend to bake a cake or
play a game like catch. Decide
on one idea for your play.

Practice what you will do.
Remember that this is a play without
words! Ask classmates to watch your play.
Can they guess what you are doing?

If You Take a Pencil by Fulvio Testa *(Dial Press, 1982)*. This book will take you on an adventure. Look at the pictures *very* carefully, and then you can draw your own story.

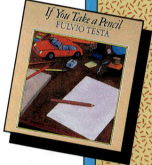

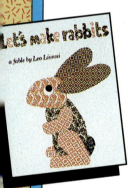

Let's Make Rabbits by Leo Lionni *(Panthean, 1982)*. A pair of scissors and a pencil make two rabbits. They become friends and have fun finding carrots.

Where the Wild Things Are Maurice Sendak *(Harper & Row, 1963)*. Max is sent to his room because he has jumped around in his wolf suit. But Max wants to go where the wild things are and become king!

A

Sue loves **animals.**

asked

admit I admit that Lani runs faster than I do.

after Jane helps around the house after school.

again It rained every day this week. It will rain again today.

always We always visit Grandma on the weekend.

animals Sue loves dogs, cats, birds, and other animals.

any Liz didn't want any milk.

anything When he was sick, Sean didn't eat anything all day.

as Janet sang as she played.

asked Mark asked for help.

awake The baby was awake all night.

away Mary went away for the day.

awake

B

---

balloon Pam bought a green balloon.

believe Do you believe that dogs can fly?

bench The old man sat on the bench.

better Jim felt better after he saw the doctor.

bigger A truck is bigger than a car.

blew The wind blew the man's hat off.

blow Lin will blow out the candles.

born The tiny kittens were born yesterday.

both Both Susan and John are six years old.

breakfast It is time for breakfast.

breaks Glass breaks if it is dropped.

bright Red and purple are bright colors.

brown The house is painted brown.

busy Ernest was busy painting the door.

balloon

blow

breaks

calf

city

closed

corncob

C

calf The cow licked her calf.

cannot The hen cannot find her eggs.

chin Alma has milk on her chin.

chinny Not by the hair on my chinny chin chin.

city They live on a farm. We live in a city.

close Abe lives close to Ruth's house.

closed This shop is closed on Sundays.

colors The drawing has many colors in it.

corncob After you eat corn, the corncob is left.

couldn't Josh couldn't go to the party.

cows These cows give lots of milk.

cried Dot cried when her puppy ran away.

curly My hair is curly, just like Mom's.

D

didn't Joe didn't like the movie.

draw Rick likes to draw trees.

drawings Jane makes drawings of cats with her pencil.

drew Jane drew four cats on her paper.

draw

E

eat Bears eat lots of fish.

else Bob is still hungry. He wants something else to eat.

emergency Call your parents if there is an emergency.

ever Will we ever get to the beach?

every We have a big picnic every summer.

everyone Everyone in my class likes to read.

eat

emergency

farm

food

friend

F

farm Carmen saw pigs and hens at the farm.

farmer The farmer lives on the farm.

fast Kim ran very fast.

finally Laura finally finished building the model.

first It was the first time that Rosa had seen snow.

flew The duck flew away.

fly I wish I could fly like a bird.

food The birds have food to eat.

friend Carmen is Juan's best friend.

from Jane walked away from the shop.

funny Julian told a funny joke.

fur My cat has very soft fur.

G

game The children made up a new game.

going Mr. Smith is going to work.

game

gone The rabbits have gone into their hole.

ground Greg planted seeds in the ground.

grow Susan wants to grow long hair like Sharon's.

ground

H

---

hair Maria likes to brush her hair.

hard It is hard to stand on your head.

heard Rob heard the dog bark.

hill Jack and Jill climbed up the hill.

hill

himself José was talking to himself.

horse The horse raced across the river.

hole The boy dug a large hole.

house That house is where I live.

hole

hurry Cathy must hurry to catch the bus.

hurts John's sore foot hurts when he walks.

hurry

ice

I

ice Everyone went skating on the ice.
ice cream Robert likes soft ice cream.

knock

J

just The cat just spilled the milk a
minute ago.

laughed

K

kinds The shop sells many kinds of
cheese.
knock Dad began to knock on the door.

leaps

L

laughed The children laughed at the
clown.
leaps The cat leaps onto the table.
liked Tom liked his new friend.

love Mary and Tom love their baby sister.

lunch Meg ate her lunch with Norma.

lunch

M

many There are many animals on a farm.

meadows The cows were eating grass in the meadows.

mind "I don't mind if I'm last in the race," said Joe.

more The kitten wanted more food.

mouse The mouse ran under the bed.

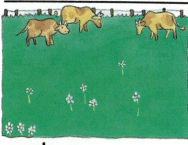

meadows

N

nest The birds made a nest.

never Alice is never late for school.

new Gail's old coat was too small. She just got a new one.

next The next bus stop is Dave's.

nice Betty made a nice gift for me.

nose My dog has a big wet nose.

nest

O

opened

old This house has been here for a long time. It is very old.

opened Father opened the letter.

orange Beth picked out a big orange pumpkin.

ouch "Ouch!" said Ed when he cut his finger.

our We live here. This is our house.

outside Mother was in the shop. We waited outside.

P

park

peaches

penny

park Lisa went to the park to play.

peaches I like to eat peaches and cream.

penny Amy put a penny in her bank.

person We need another person for our team.

pictures Clara draws pictures of dogs in her art class.

please "Please, can I go out to play?" asked Amanda.

pocket Mr. Long's pen is in his pocket.

police The police helped the lost boy.

popped The big soap bubble popped.

pretended Pat pretended she was a tree during the school play.

pulls Ed pulls his toy across the room.

puppies All the puppies are asleep.

purple Sara has a purple dress.

pushed Todd pushed the door open.

puppies

R

race

rabbits Rabbits like to eat carrots.

race Chuck won the race.

rainbow You may see a rainbow if it rains as the sun comes out.

read Nan will read to the class.

Bill read yesterday.

riding I see Ted riding his bike.

room This room is the bedroom.

rainbow

read

sandwiches

sheep

sitting

snuggles

round A ball is round.

rude Sam never says " please" or " thank you." He is very rude.

running My father goes running every morning.

S

---

sandwiches I like to eat sandwiches for lunch.

sheep The sheep are on the hill.

show Bob will show you how to swim.

sitting Sara was sitting on her bed.

small The big cat picked up the small kitten.

snow We get cold when we play in the snow.

snuggles The kitten snuggles up to his mother.

some Liz picked some flowers.

soon It is late . I want to go home soon .

spinach Eating spinach is good for you .

stairs Jo ran up the stairs .

start The race is ready to start .

stays A pine tree stays green all year .

still The dentist told Jack to sit still .

stop You must stop for the red light .

stories Joe liked all the stories his father read to him .

story My mother reads me a story before I go to bed .

straw Cows and horses eat straw .

string Mike tied up the box with string .

strong The strong man lifted the big box .

sure Tom is sure that he is six years old .

ready to **start**

Mother reads a **story.**

straw

T

---

television Nancy watches television in the morning .

thanks "Thanks for the gift," said Sue .

string

things

thinking

threw

Dad **told** me.

their We went to see our grandpa and grandma. Their house is smaller than ours.

them I like Fran and Mike. I want to be friends with them.

there We went to the beach. It was warm there.

these That book is not mine. These books are mine.

things I like to make things out of clay.

thinking Harriet was thinking about her new pet.

thought Robin thought of a gift for Tom.

three There were three little pigs.

threw Andy threw the ball to his sister.

tired After playing all day, Rosa felt very tired.

today Today is Sunday.

together All of us finished the race together.

told Dad told me about the large birds.

tomorrow Today is Sunday. Tomorrow will be Monday.

took We took a walk with the dog.

tried Jim tried to catch the bus.

true It is true that ducks can fly.

turtles Turtles can swim very well.

tyrannosaurus Bob likes the movie about the big, green tyrannosaurus.

two The dish broke into two pieces.

turtles

U

under Ron sleeps under the blankets.

until We can play until it gets dark.

two pieces

V

vegetables The vegetables I like best are carrots and green beans.

very An ant is very small.

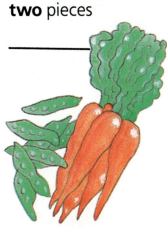

vegetables

W

wait Greg has to wait for the bus.

walk Grandpa takes a walk every day.

Greg must **wait.**

watch

winked

Pedro **won**
the contest.

want Do you want more vegetables?

wanted Yesterday, I wanted to go to the playground.

warm The sun feels warm.

watch The cat likes to watch birds.

were Three birds were sitting in the tree.

when The dog barks when we come home.

where I live here. Where do you live?

why Jim wanted to know why snow is white.

winked Joan winked at her brother as she told the joke.

wise Grandma knows everything. She is very wise.

won Pedro won the fishing contest.

won't The dog and the cat won't play together.

work The toy truck broke. It does not work any more.

world The ship sailed around the world.

would Anna has a big sandwich. She would like to share it with Jeff.

wrong When Dad took a wrong turn, he lost his way.

The toy truck does not **work**.

Y

---

yellow The color of my cat is bright yellow.

you'll I will lend you my bat if you'll lend me your ball.

Anna **would** like to share.

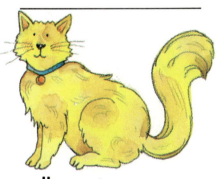

yellow cat

213

WORD LIST

The following story critical words appear in *Make a Wish*. The words are listed next to the number of the page on which they first appear.

Unit 1

A Morning in Fall

11 farm
when
still

12 stays
warm

13 cows

15 calf

16 sheep

Who Took the Farmer's Hat?

22 farmer
old
brown
took
away

24 hole

26 nest
nice

28 new

A Rainbow for Sara

32 asked
string

33 you'll

34 thinking

36 orange
yellow
purple

38 rainbow

Polar Bear Leaps

47 born
first
snow

48 as
small
ice
breaks

50 leaps

The Three Little Pigs

56 three

57 straw
house
strong

58 knock
friend

59 blow

60 blew

A World of Animals

69 world
animals
under
ground

70 turtles

72 rabbits
meadows

The Hare and the Tortoise

76 walk
city
park

77 fast

78 race

79 very
stop

82 won

214

215

These authors have written some of the stories in this book.

DOROTHY ALDIS

DOROTHY ALDIS

Dorothy Aldis wrote many books, poems, and stories for young people. Her first book also had songs in it. Dorothy Aldis also wrote a true story. It was about the life of Beatrix Potter, who wrote the Peter Rabbit stories. As a young girl, she moved from Chicago to a farm. *(1896–1966)*

ROWENA BENNETT

Rowena Bennett has written poems and plays for children. Her poems have been part of collections of poetry. She wrote about animals, people, and the world around us. Her writing has been enjoyed by many readers. *(Born 1896)*

AILEEN FISHER

Aileen Fisher has written many poems and stories. She has won awards for her writing. Aileen Fisher says she has always loved the country. She grew up in the country. Now she lives in Colorado near a mountain. She likes to take a walk every day with her dog along the mountain trails. *(Born 1906)*

AILEEN FISHER

ELOISE GREENFIELD

ELOISE GREENFIELD

Eloise Greenfield did not think she would be a writer when she grew up. She says, "I loved words, but I loved to read them, not write them. I loved their sounds." Now writing is an important part of her life. Eloise Greenfield has received the American Library Association Notable Book Award and many other awards. *(Born 1929)*

STEVEN KROLL

STEVEN KROLL

Steven Kroll says, "I really love writing for children." When he writes, he tries to remember things about his own childhood. "When I write about a child's room, that room is often my own." He thinks it is important for writers to remember what it was like to be a child. *(Born 1941)*

ARNOLD LOBEL

Arnold Lobel wrote and illustrated books for children. His books have won many awards. One thing he especially liked about being a writer was being able to make a character do just what he wanted it to do. *(1933–1987)*

ARNOLD LOBEL

MARIANNA MAYER

Marianna Mayer is a writer and illustrator. When she was little, she drew pictures for stories that her parents read to her. She decided to become an artist. She likes to illustrate fairy tales. She says working on fairy tales is "wonderful—they are my friends." *(Born 1945)*

MARIANNA MAYER

MERCER MAYER

MERCER MAYER

Mercer Mayer is an author and illustrator. He has won many awards for his books. His first book was *A Boy, a Dog, and a Frog.* It was made into a movie. Mercer Mayer does not think of his books as being only for children. He says, "My books are for the children in all of us, really." *(Born 1943)*

DAVID McPHAIL

DAVID McPHAIL

David McPhail illustrates books for children. He also writes books. David McPhail says he does not know what a picture will look like when he begins to draw it. "I have the feeling that if I could see very clearly what I wanted from the beginning, there would be no reason for me to draw." He is a Caldecott winner. *(Born 1940)*

A. A. MILNE

Alan Alexander Milne wrote many stories and poems for children. Some of the stories are about a boy named Christopher Robin and a bear named Winnie-the-Pooh. A. A. Milne had one son. His name was also Christopher Robin. *(1882–1956)*

A. A. MILNE

JOAN NŎDSET

Joan Nŏdset has written many books for children. She gets her ideas for her stories from different places. The idea for one of her books came from a dream she had. When she was growing up, her mother read to her almost every night. Joan Nŏdset says she wanted to be a writer for as long as she can remember.

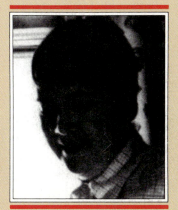

JOAN NŎDSET

JACK PRELUTSKY

Jack Prelutsky has written many books and poems for children. He was born in New York City where he went to the High School for Music and Art. He sings opera and has worked as a singer, actor, and poet. His poems for children are clever and funny. He writes about people he knows and himself.

MIKE THALER

Mike Thaler writes children's books. He also illustrates books. He has written more than sixty children's books. Some of his books are collections of riddles, jokes, and cartoons. Mike Thaler is also a songwriter and a sculptor.
(Born 1936)

AUTHOR INDEX

"How to Help Make a Bird's Nest" by Marion de Barenne, © 1989 by Silver, Burdett & Ginn Inc.

"I Want to Be Big, NOW!" written and illustrated by Bernard Wiseman, © 1989 by Silver, Burdett & Ginn Inc.

"Lee Bennett Hopkins Interviews David McPhail," © 1989 by Silver, Burdett & Ginn Inc.

Me and My Flying Machine by Marianna Mayer, illustrated by Mercer Mayer. Copyright © 1971 by Marianna Mayer and Mercer Mayer. Adapted and reprinted by permission of Scholastic Inc.

"Melissa's Friend Kim" by Christel Kleitsch, adapted from Head In, Head Out. Copyright © 1984 by Ginn & Co. Reprinted by permission of Ginn & Co., Canada.

"Mercy, Percy" by Else Holmelund Minarik, © 1989 by Silver, Burdett & Ginn Inc.

"A Morning in Fall" specially written by Reeve Lindberg for Silver, Burdett & Ginn Inc. Text © 1989 by Reeve Lindberg, photographs © 1989 by Richard W. Brown.

Polar Bear Leaps by Derek Hall, illustrated by John Butler. Text copyright © 1985 by Derek Hall. Illustrations copyright © 1985 John Butler. First published by Walker Books Limited. By permission of Walker Books Limited.

"A Rainbow for Sara" by Jane Mechling, © 1989 by Silver, Burdett & Ginn Inc.

"Scramble" from A Gopher in the Garden by Jack Prelutsky, copyright © 1966, 1967 by Jack Prelutsky. Reprinted by permission of the author.

"The Story Game" adapted from The Tyrannosaurus Game by Steven Kroll, illustrated by Rick Kolding based on original illustrations by Tomie dePaola. Text copyright © 1976 by Steven Kroll. Original illustrations copyright © 1976 by Tomie dePaola. All rights reserved. Reprinted by permission of Holiday House.

"Then" By Dorothy Aldis, reprinted by permission of G.P. Putnam's Sons from Hop, Skip and Jump! by Dorothy Aldis, copyright 1934, copyright renewed © 1961 by Dorothy Aldis.

"The Three Little Pigs" adapted by Adam Burdick, © 1989 by Silver, Burdett & Ginn Inc.

"Under a Stone" from Out in the Dark and Daylight by Aileen Fisher. Text copyright © 1980 by Aileen Fisher. Reprinted by permission of Harper & Row, Publishers, Inc., and of Aileen Fisher.

"When You Talk to a Monkey" from The Day Is Dancing by Rowena Bennett, copyright 1948, © 1968 by Rowena Bastin Bennett. Reprinted by permission of Modern Curriculum Press, Inc.

"The Wishing Well" from Mouse Tales by Arnold Lobel, copyright © 1972 by Arnold Lobel. Text and art reprinted by permission of Harper & Row, Publishers, Inc.

"A World of Animals" by Susan Schroeder, © 1989 by Silver, Burdett & Ginn Inc.

Who Took the Farmer's Hat? by Joan Nôdset. Text copyright 1963 by Joan L. Nôdset. Reprinted by permission of Harper & Row, Publishers, Inc.

BOOKS TO ENJOY

Page 101: Jacket art from The Cat in the Hat by Dr. Seuss, © 1957 by Dr. Seuss, © renewed 1985 by Theodore S. Geisel. Reprinted by permission of Random House, Inc.

Page 101: Jacket art from Demi's Find the Animal A·B·C by Demi, copyright © 1985 by Demi. Published by Grossett & Dunlap, Inc., a division of The Putnam Publishing Group.

Page 101: Jacket art from 17 Kings and 42 Elephants by Margaret Mahy, pictures by Patricia MacCarthy. Pictures © 1987 by Patricia MacCarthy. Published by Dial Books for Young Readers.

Page 197: Jacket art from If You Take a Pencil by Fulvio Testa. Copyright © 1982 by Fulvio Testa. Reproduced by permission of the American publisher, Dial Books for Young Readers, and of the British publisher, Andersen Press Ltd.

Page 197: Jacket art from Let's Make Rabbits by Leo Lionni, copyright © 1982 by Leo Lionni. Reprinted by permission of Pantheon Books, a division of Random House, Inc.

Page 197: Jacket art from Where the Wild Things Are by Maurice Sendak, copyright © 1963 by Maurice Sendak. Reproduced by permission of the American publisher, Harper & Row, Publishers, Inc., and of the British publisher, The Bodley Head Ltd.

TIME OUT FOR BOOKS

Art from Leo the Late Bloomer by Robert Kraus, pictures by José Aruego. Illustrations copyright © 1971 by José Aruego. Reprinted by permission of Simon & Schuster, Inc.

Art from The Snowy Day by Ezra Jack Keats, © Ezra Jack Keats, 1962. Reprinted by permission of Viking Penguin Inc.

COVER: Maryjane Begin

DESIGN: Design Five, NYC and Kirchoff/Wohlberg in cooperation with Silver Burdett & Ginn

ILLUSTRATION: 4, Ron Lehen; 5, (t) Muntes, (bl) Dennis Hockerman, (br) Susan David; 6, (t) John Wallner, (b) Richard Kolding; 7, (t) John Wallner, (b) Dora Leder; 20, Michelle Fridkin; 21, Dennis Hockerman; 22–28, Dennis Hockerman; 29 Susan Jaekel; 30–31, (tl) from Animal Alphabet by Bert Kitchen, copyright © by Bert Kitchen, reproduced by permission of the publisher, Dial Books for Young Readers and Lutterworth Press, (tr) from The Complete Nonsense of Edward Lear, edited and introduced by Holbrook Jackson, Dover Publications, Inc., (bl) from All About Arthur by Eric Carle, copyright © 1974, (br) from Alphabatics by Suse MacDonald, copyright © 1986 by Suse MacDonald, reproduced with permission of Bradbury Press, an Affiliate of Macmillan, Inc.; 32–38, Kathleen Howell; 39, Christa Kieffer; 40–43, Susan David; 44–45, Pat Hoggan; 46–52, John Butler; 46, Vincente Roso; 53, Susan Jaekel; 54–55, Richard Kolding; 56–64, Mask Construction by Bob Barner; 65, Susan Jaekel; 66–67, Michael Halbert; 68–74, Susan David; 76–82, Ron Lehen; 84–85, Teresa Harmon; 85, Susan Jaekel; 86–97, Diane Magnuson; 100, Sharron O'Neil; 104–110, Bernard Wiseman; 112–113, Dora Leder; 114–122, Arnold Lobel; 124, Arnold Lobel; 125, Bill Morrison; 126–139, Illustrated by Rick Kolding, based on original illustrations by Tomie dePaola in "The Tyrannosaurus Game" © 1976 by Tomie dePaola; 140–141, Diane and Leo Dillon; 142–150, Maxie Chambliss; 151, Susan Jaekel; 152–153, Paul Turnbaugh; 154, Floyd Cooper; 157, David McPhail; 159, Susan Jaekel; 160–168, David McPhail; 170–171, Stan Tusan; 172–179, Karen Loccisano; 180–181, Teresa Harmon; 182–193, Marianna & Mercer Mayer; 196, Susan Jaekel; 198, Tom Sperling; 199, Richard Kolding, Cheryl Kirk Noll, Tom Sperling; 200, Bob Barner, Richard Kolding, Cheryl Kirk Noll; 201, Bob Barner, Richard Kolding, Cheryl Kirk Noll; 202, Bob Barner, Cheryl Kirk Noll, Tom Sperling; 203, Richard Kolding, Cheryl Kirk Noll; 204, Bob Barner, Richard Kolding, Cheryl Kirk Noll, Tom Sperling; 205, Bob Barner, Richard Kolding, Cheryl Kirk Noll; 206, Richard Kolding, Cheryl Kirk Noll, Tom Sperling; 207, Richard Kolding, Cheryl Kirk Noll, Tom Sperling; 208, Richard Kolding, Cheryl Kirk Noll, Tom Sperling; 209, Bob Barner, Richard Kolding, Cheryl Kirk Noll; 210, Richard Kolding, Cheryl Kirk Noll, Tom Sperling; 211, Bob Barner, Richard Kolding; 212, Bob Barner, Richard Kolding, Cheryl Kirk Noll; 213, Bob Barner, Cheryl Kirk Noll, Tom Sperling.

PHOTOGRAPHY: 8, Gary Sinick; 10–18, Richard W. Brown; 20, Richard W. Brown; 41–43, Lawrence Migdale; 56–64, Stephen Ogilvy; 102, reproduced by kind permission of New Cavendish Books from The Art of the Tin Toy by David Pressland; 152–153, Carlos Vergara; 155–156 & 158, David Niles; 216, Mike Thaler; 217 (b) Harper & Row; 218, (t) Harper & Row, (b) Holiday House; 219, (b) Dial/Dutton; 220, (t) Western Publishing, (b) H.W. Wilson Co.; 221, (b) Nunawading Gazette.

C D E F G H I J—VHP—97 96 95 94 93 92 91

Willow Field Elementary
3900 Route 31
Liverpool, New York   13090